The Tao of Bondage

An Erotic Binding Companion

Nell Gwyn

DRRTY GRRL PRODUCTIONS

The Tao of Bondage
An Erotic Binding Companion

Drrty Grrl Productions

Hardcover ISBN: 9781946732620
Softcover ISBN: 9781946732798

Copyright © 2019 Nell Gwyn

All rights reserved. No part of this book may be reproduced in any form or by any means, electronic, mechanical, digital, photocopying or recording, except for the inclusion in a review, without permission in writing from the publisher.

The Tao of Naughty series is presented by:

DRRTY GRRL PRODUCTIONS

Erotic Exploration & Empowerment

more than the limbs.

Immobilizing the body

enlivens the soul.

Gags, subdue

Marks left by bonds are

a temporary brand.

Flexibility enhances

Blindfolds blinker

the act of binding is

The struggle for release is

its own reward.

Binding under clothes is

Hobbling

One zip strip can carry

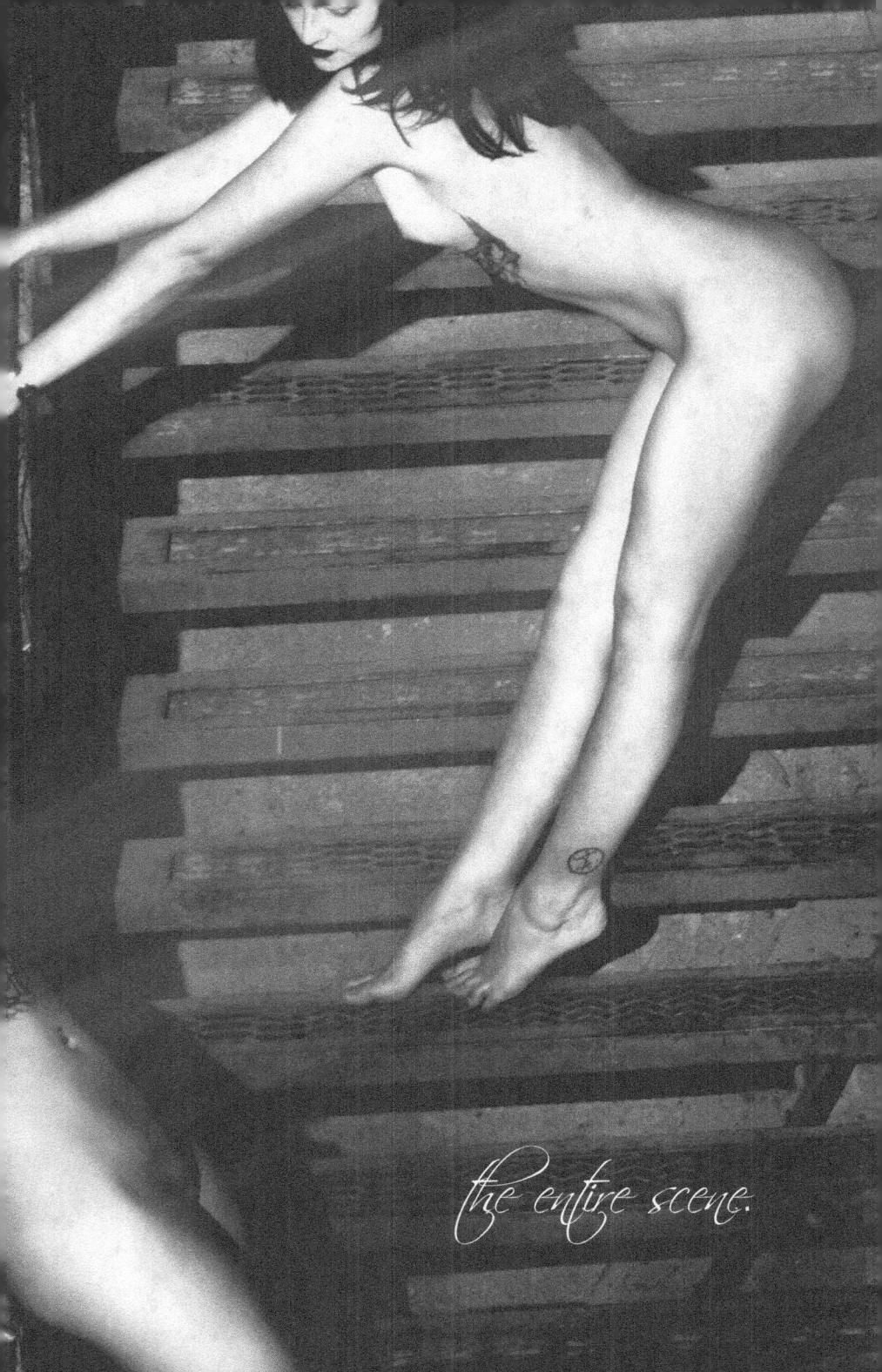

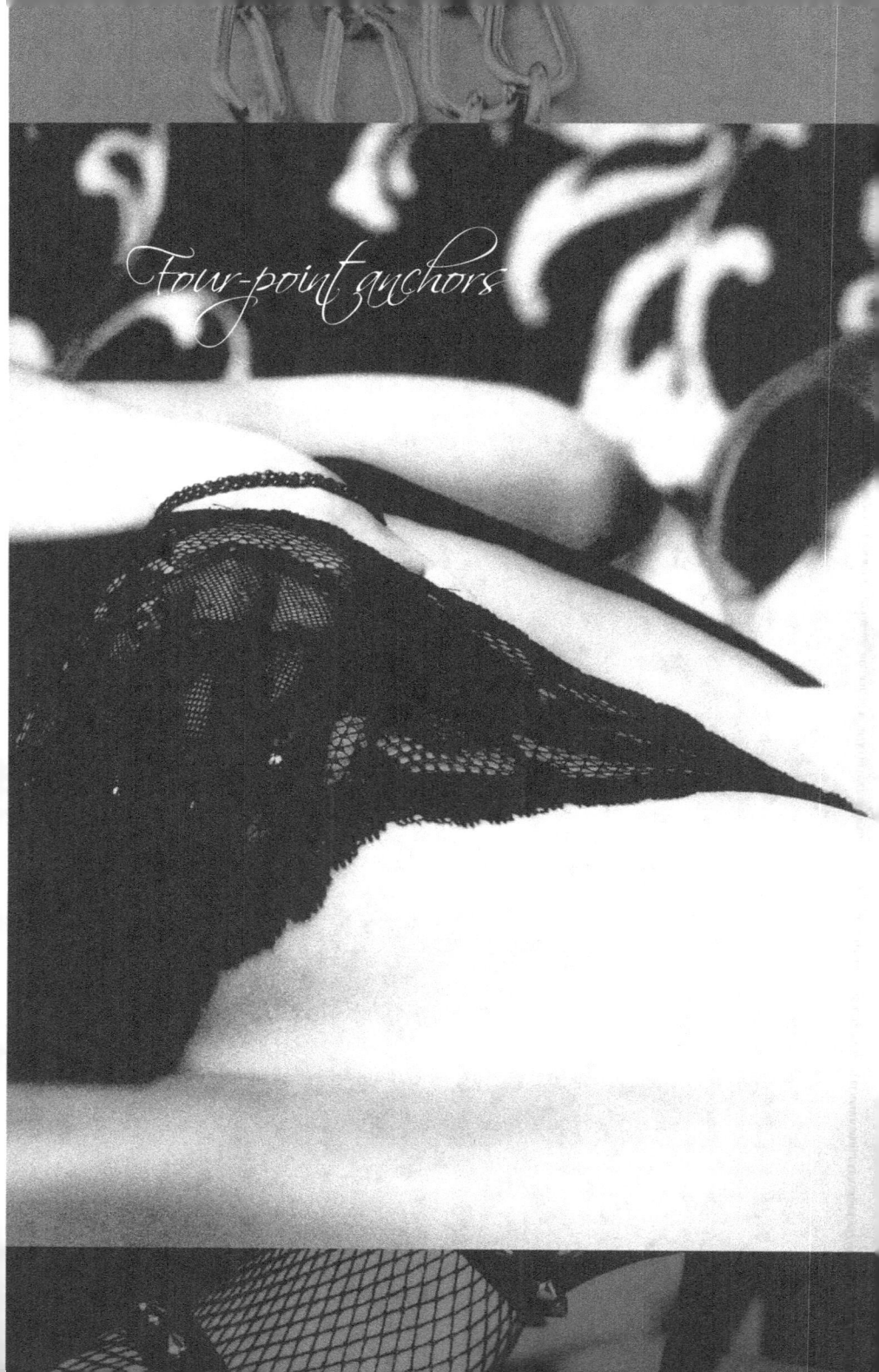

The rigging is less important

than the rigger.

Crotch ropes

Total trust allows for

total vulnerability

During bondage,

soul binds to soul.

Words restrict will.

Strapping on cuffs

Bindings are ribbons

that wrap the gift.

Breast bondage

highlights, beauty

Belly chains are

the ultimate accessory.

The knots are as important

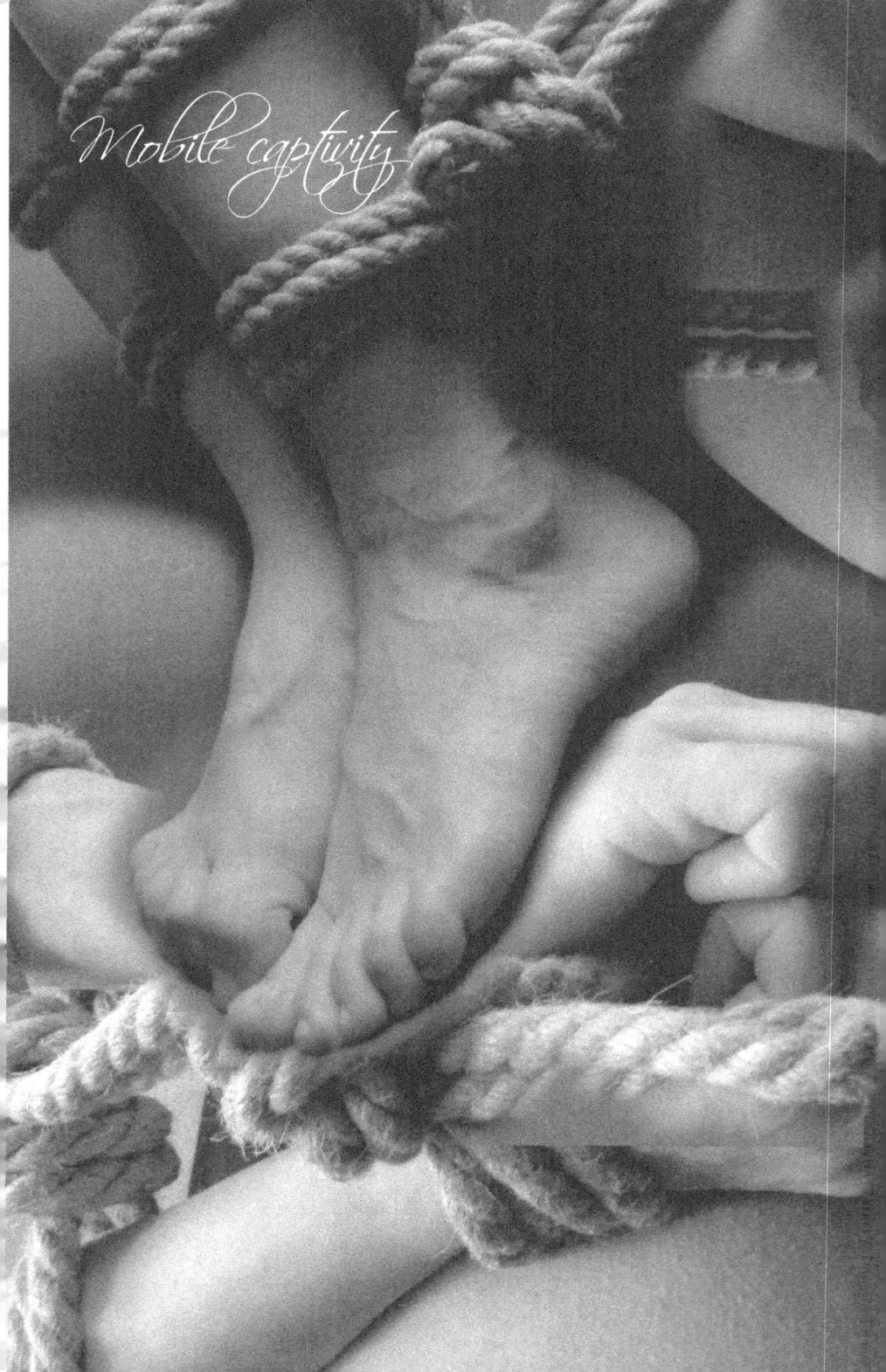

expands possibilities.

A patient application

A harness is a handle

and an anchor.

Being ensnared

is enlightening.

Subduing the body

subdues the mind.

Spreader bars

Aesthetics are

A chastity belt

Corsets limit

The Tao of Naughty Series

The Tao of Sex
An Erotic Bedside Companion

The Tao of Bondage
An Erotic Binding Companion

The Tao of BDSM
An Erotic Playtime Companion

www.ingramcontent.com/pod-product-compliance
Lightning Source LLC
Chambersburg PA
CBHW050203130526
44591CB00034B/2073